® Honey Bear Books is a trademark owned by Honey Bear
Productions, Inc., and is registered in the U.S. Patent and
Trademark Office. All Rights Reserved.
ISBN: 0-87449-141-X
Published by Modern Publishing, a division of Unisystems, Inc.

Printed in Korea

# CONTENTS

# THE GOLD STAR
# NUMBERS, SHAPES AND COLORS BOOK

MODERN PUBLISHING
A Division of Unisystems, Inc.
New York, New York 10022

# NUMBERS

1

1 fish

1 duck

1 pig

1 ice cream cone

1 parrot

1 orange

1 flower

1 leaf

1 frog

1 pot

1 apple

1 pencil

2

2 puppie[s]

2 mushrooms

2 ducklings

1 2

8

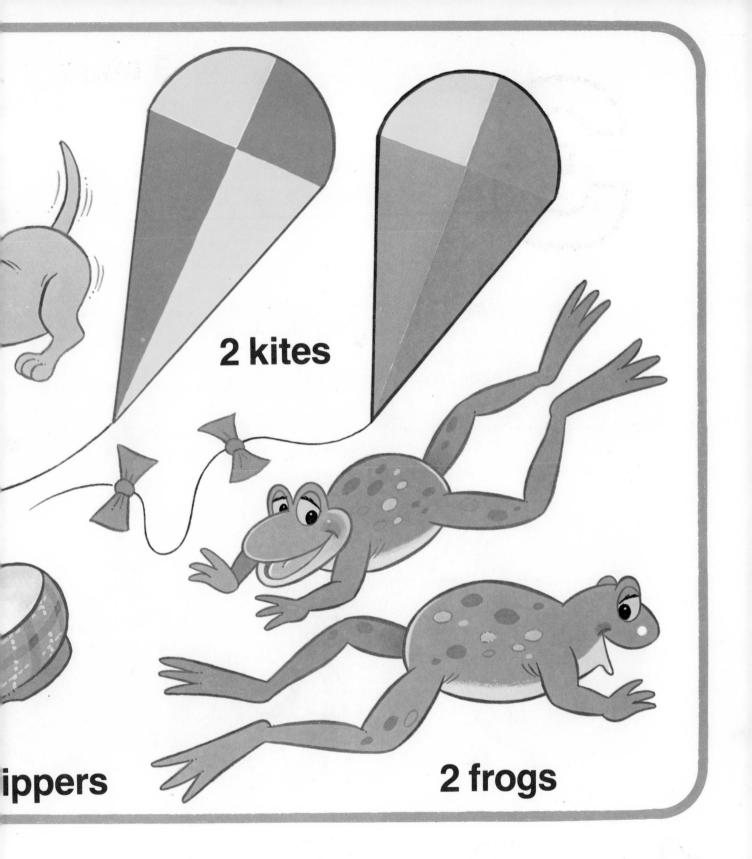

2 kites

ippers

2 frogs

9

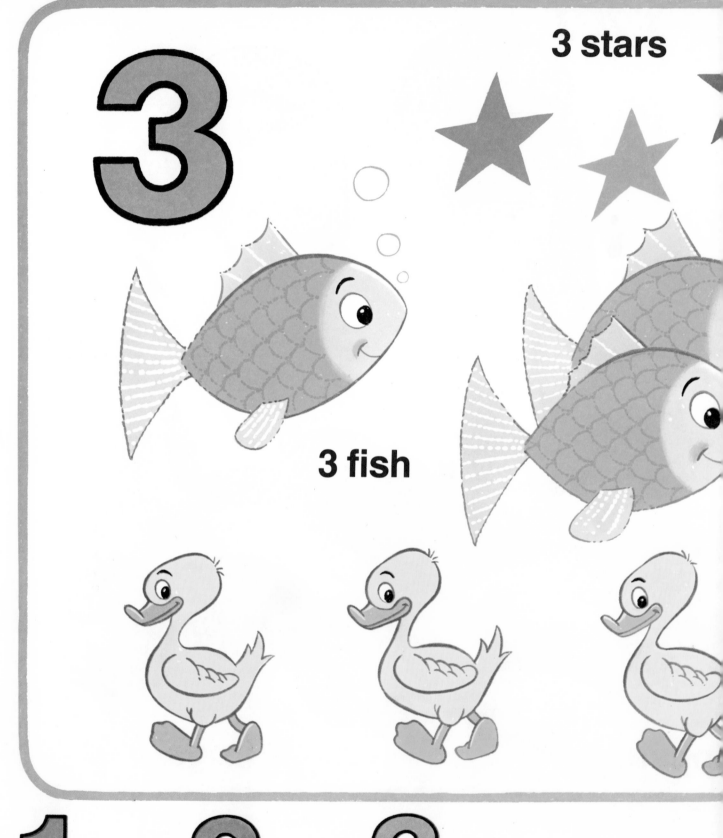

3 stars

3 fish

3

1 2 3

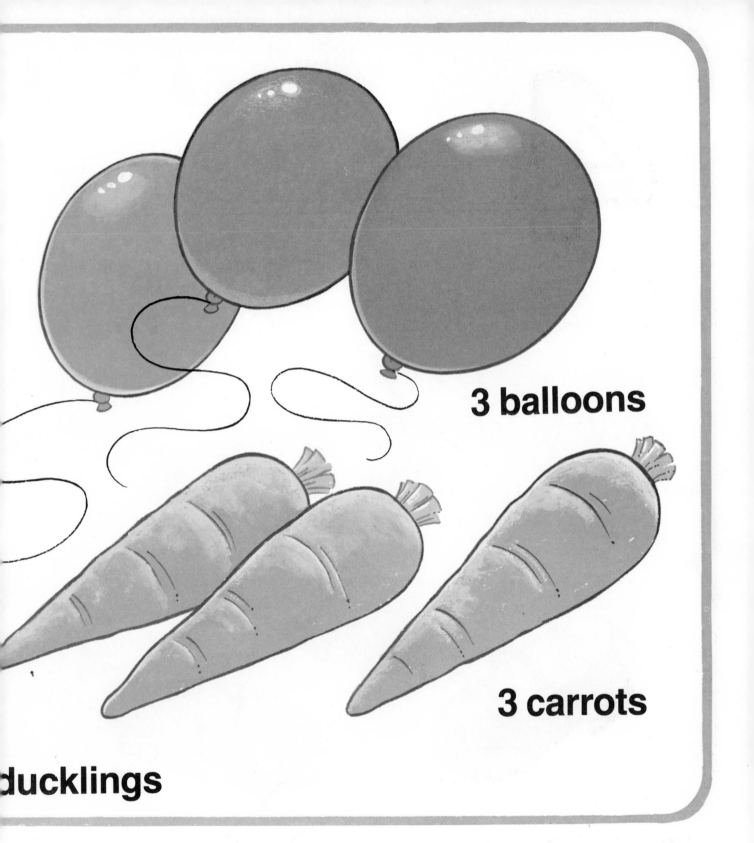

**3 balloons**

**3 carrots**

ducklings

4

4 shoes

1 2 3 4

12

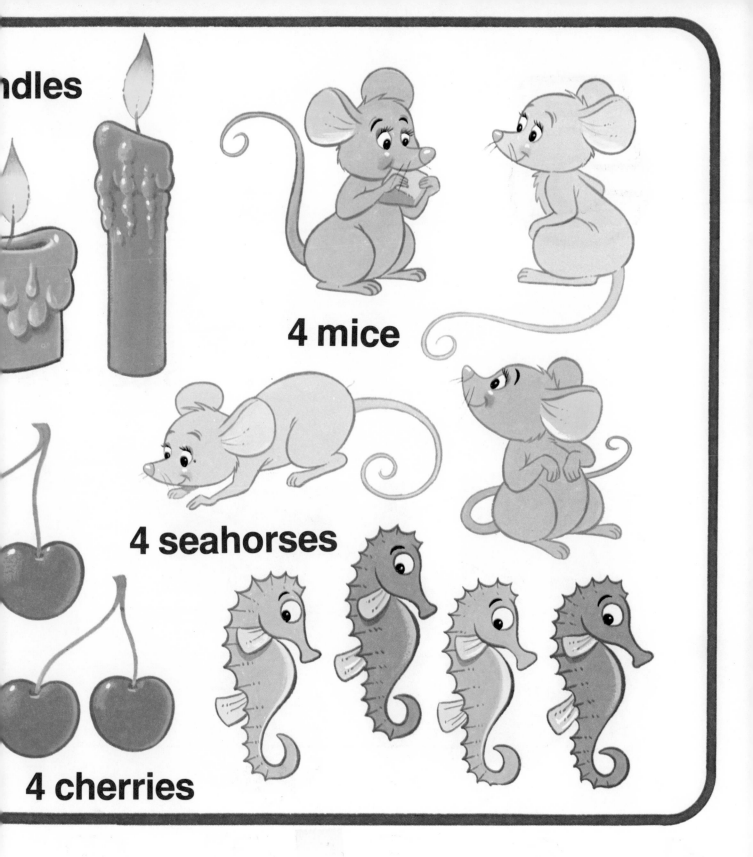

ndles

4 mice

4 seahorses

4 cherries

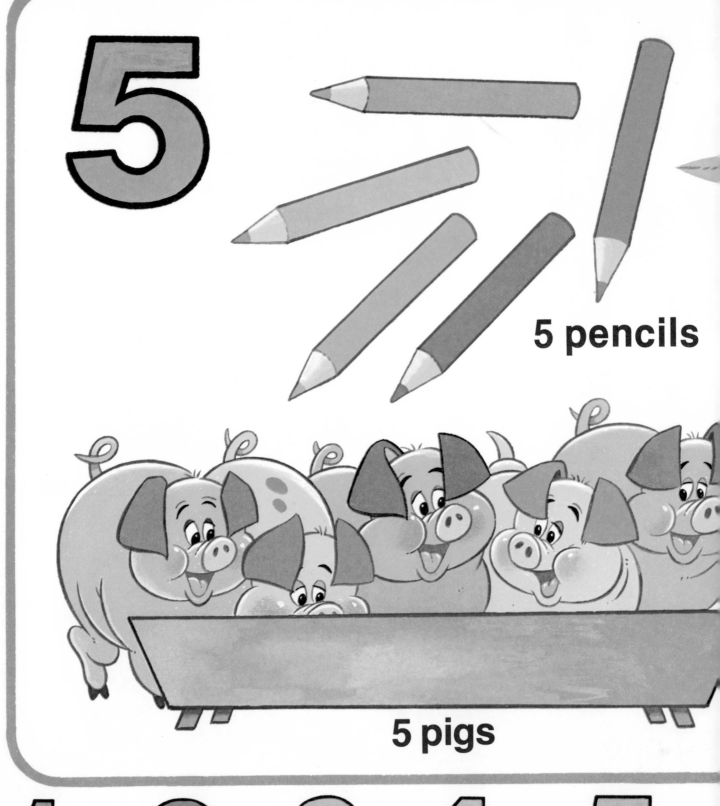

5 pencils

5 pigs

5

1 2 3 4 5

**5 birds**

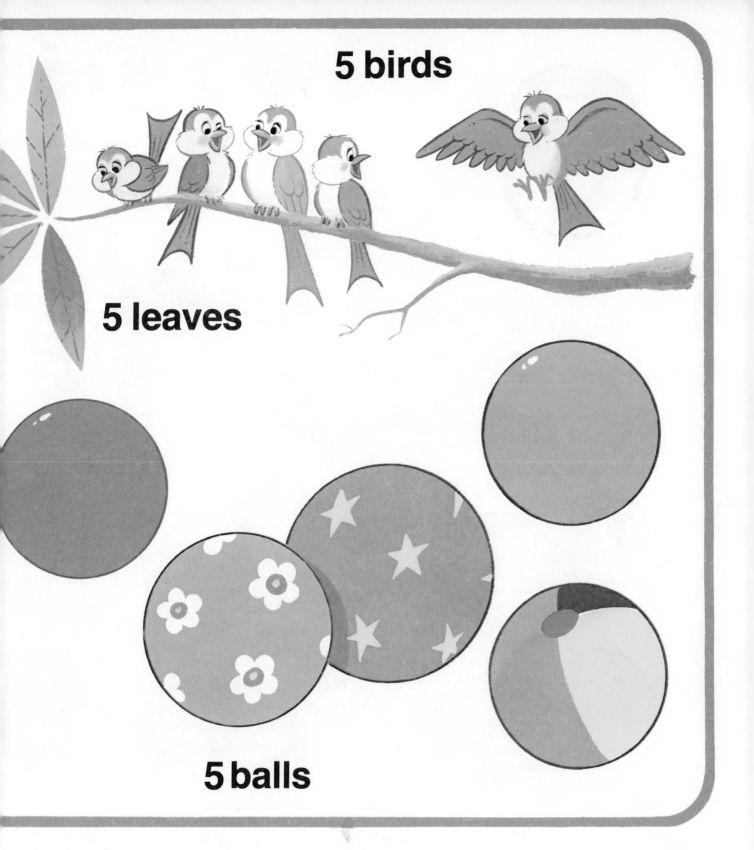

**5 leaves**

**5 balls**

6 turtles

6

1 2 3 4 5

16

**6 puppies**

**6 hats**

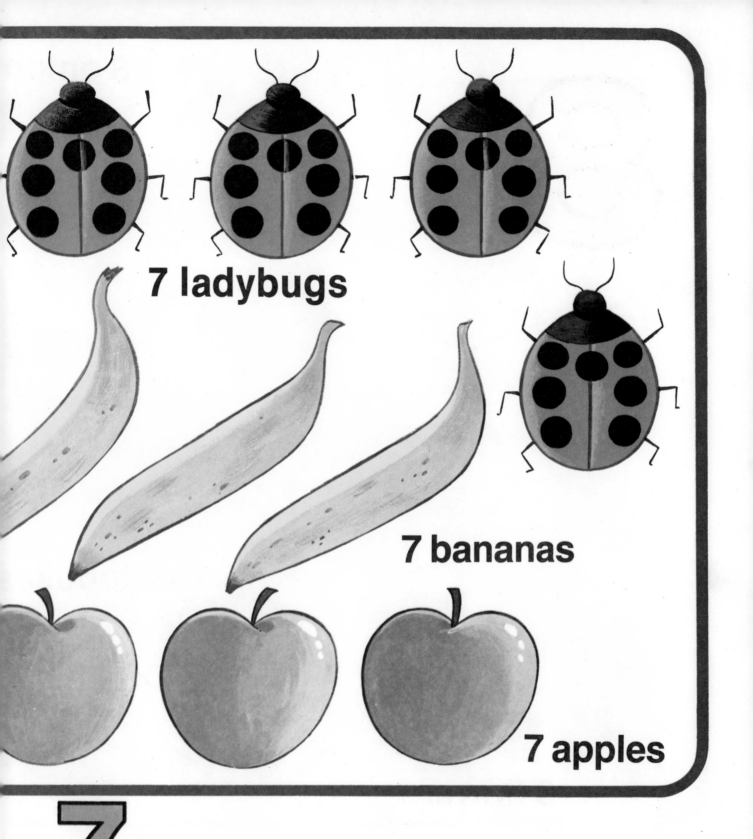

**7 ladybugs**

**7 bananas**

**7 apples**

7

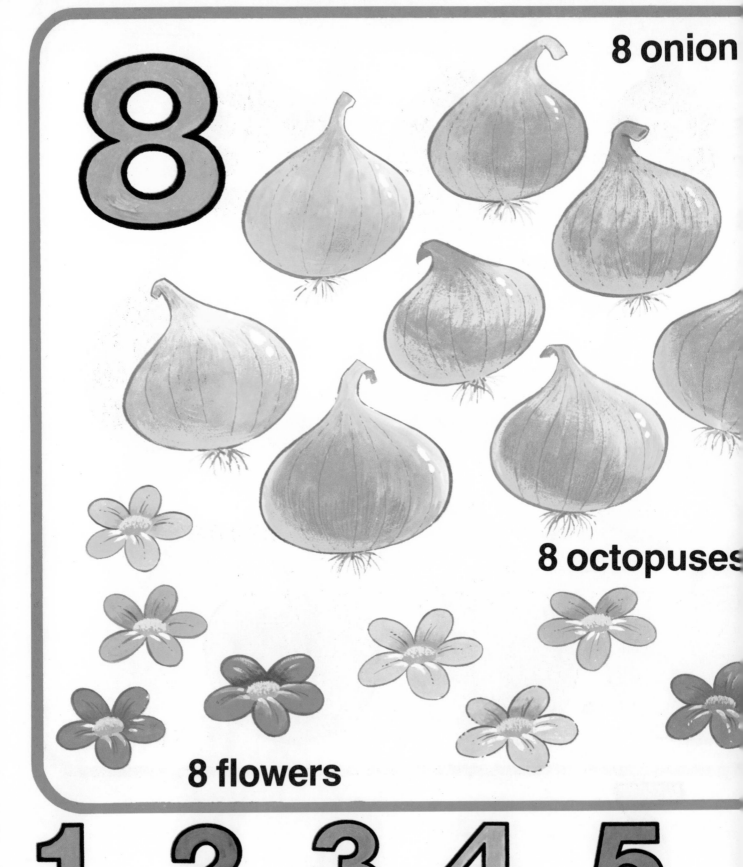

**8**

8 onion

8 octopuses

8 flowers

1 2 3 4 5

20

7 8

# 9

9 paint brushes

9 stars

1 2 3 4 5

**9 cupcakes**

7 8 9

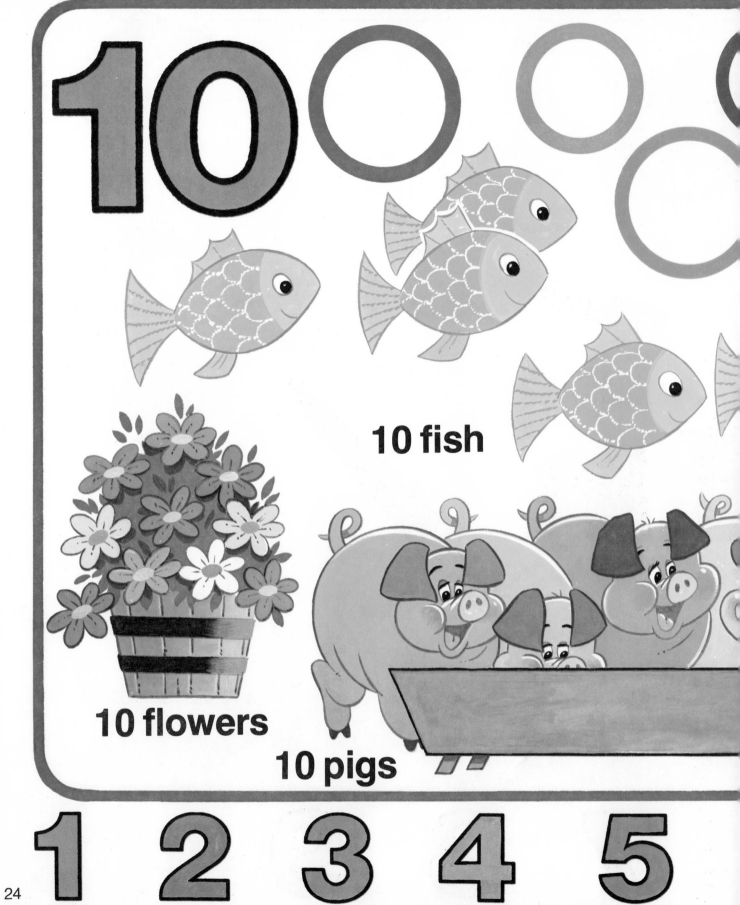

10 fish

10 flowers

10 pigs

1 2 3 4 5

24

# 10 rings

7 8 9 10

# SHAPES

**Rings**

**Squares**

**Circles**

**Rectangles**

**Triangles are shapes with three sides.**

**2 triangles can make a square.**

**2 triangles can make a rectangle.**

**2 triangles can make a diamond.**

**Many triangles can make a rectangle.**

**2 triangles can make a 6 pointed star.**

30

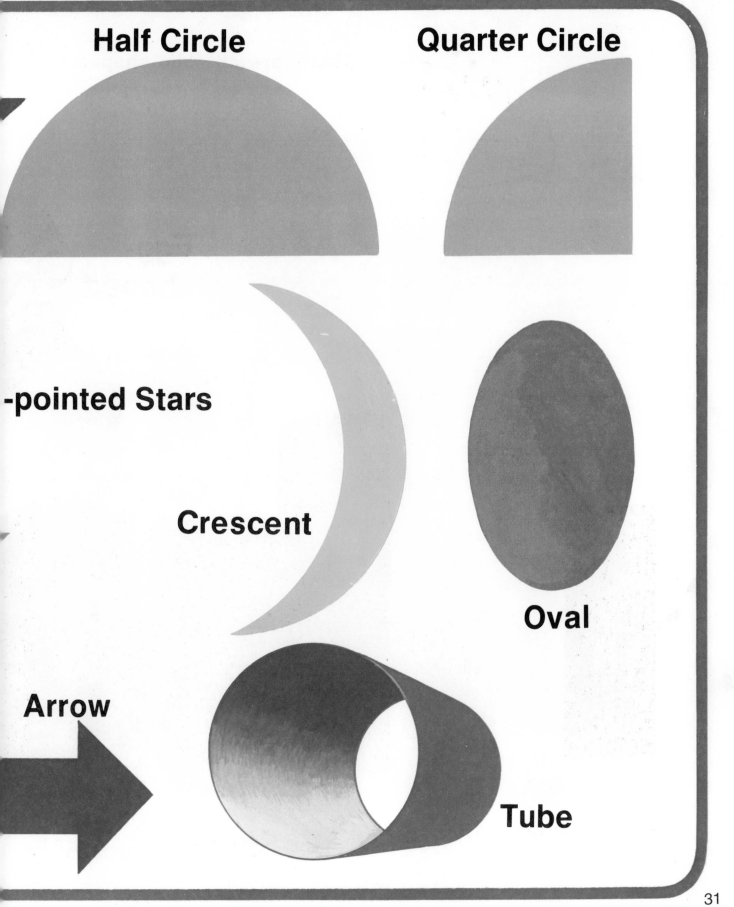

**Half Circle**

**Quarter Circle**

**-pointed Stars**

**Crescent**

**Oval**

**Arrow**

**Tube**

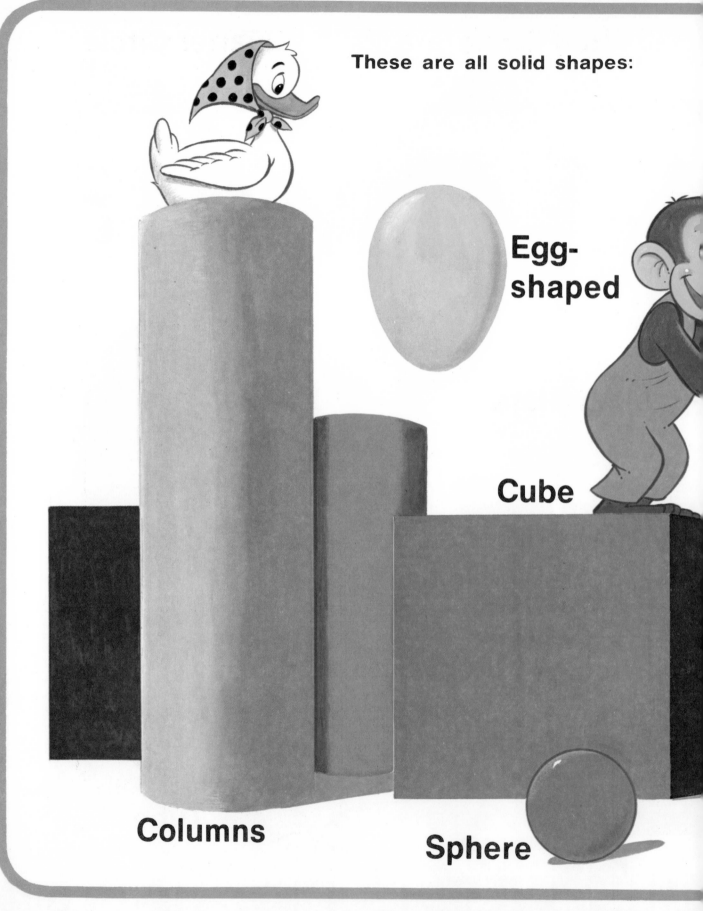

These are all solid shapes:

Egg-shaped

Cube

Columns

Sphere

32

**Pyramid**

**Sphere**

**Blocks**

33

**Here are many shapes together.**

**When you play card games these are the shapes you will find on playing cards:**

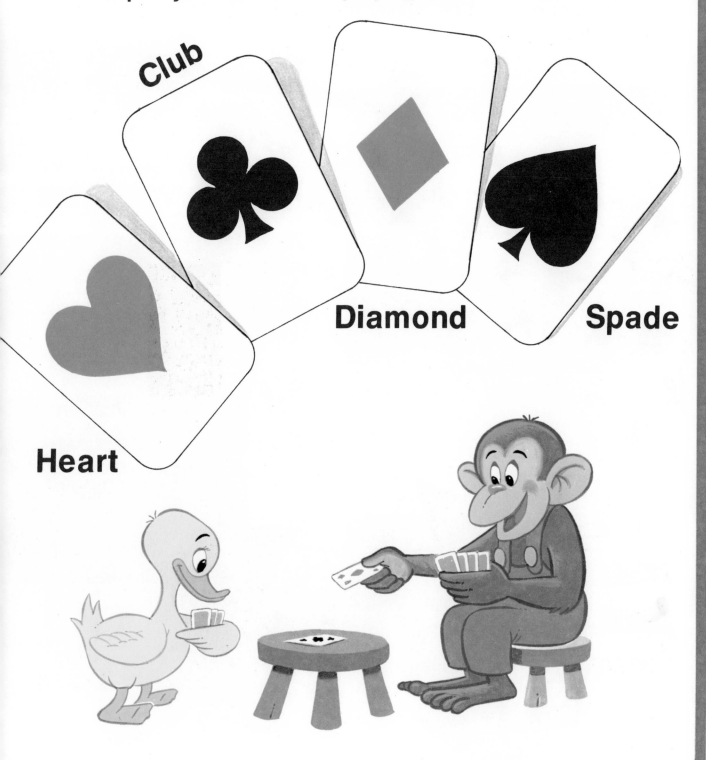

Club

Diamond

Spade

Heart

Here are some objects to draw using rectangles, circles, stars, triangles, squares and a crescent.

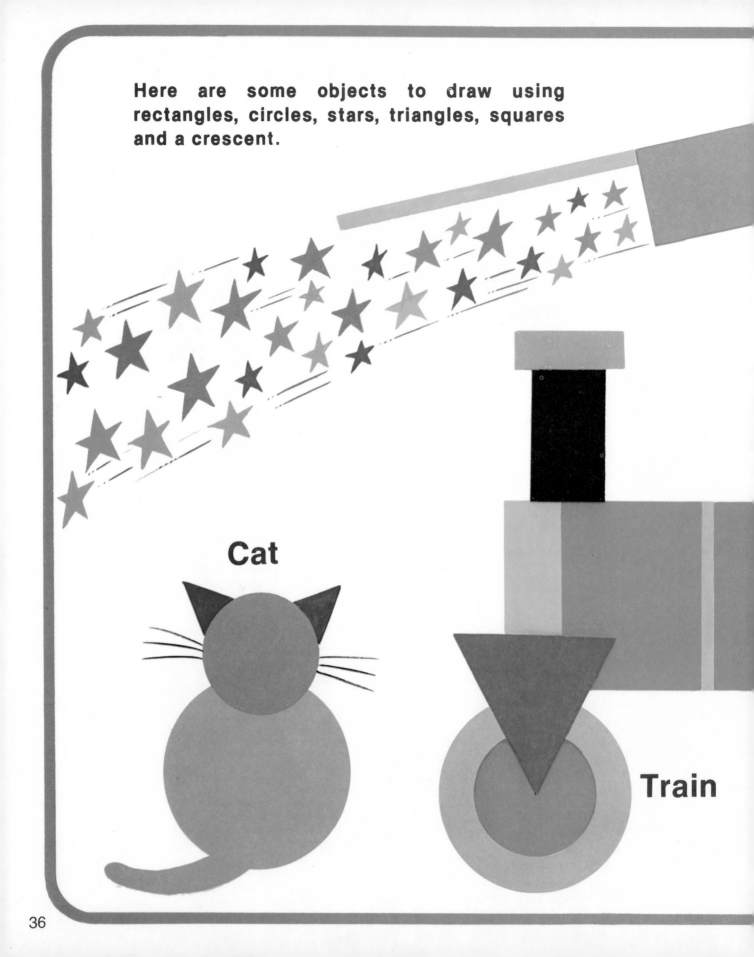

**Cat**

**Train**

**Rocket**

**Man in the Moon**

**House**

# A Funny Man

## A Singing Cat

## A Colorful Caterpillar

# A Happy Clown

## A Smiling Cat

# COLORS

When the sun shines through the rain it makes a lovely colorful rainbow.

1 Red

2 Orange

3 Yellow

1

2

3

4

4 Green

5 Blue

6 Indigo

7 Violet

5

6

7

# Primary Colors

Red

Yellow

Blue

# Secondary Colors

**Red and yellow make orange.**

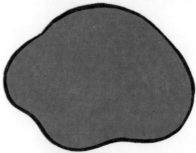

**Blue and yellow make green.**

Blue and red make purple.

**Red, yellow, and blue make brown.**

**All these colors are seen every day—try to learn them.**

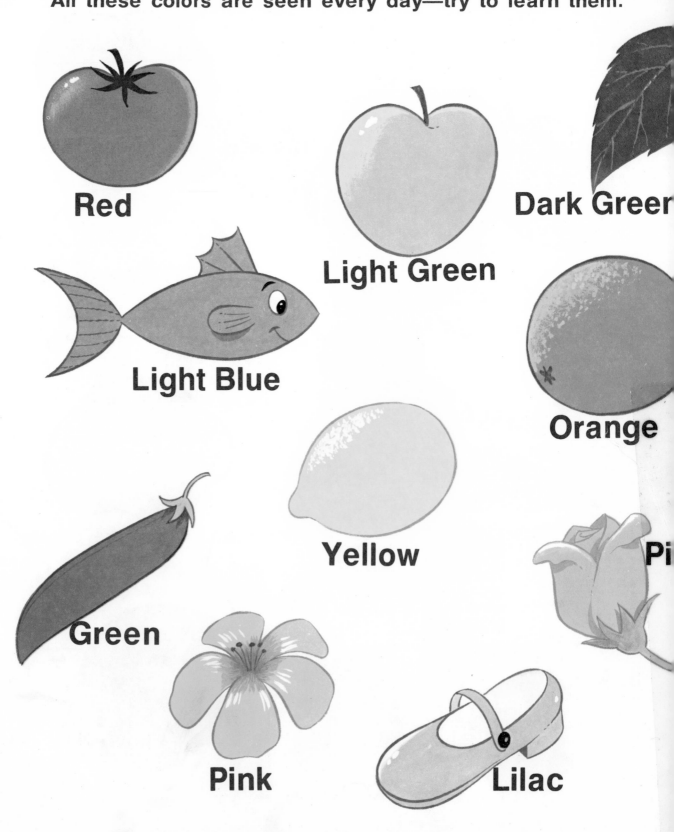

Red

Light Green

Dark Green

Light Blue

Orange

Yellow

Green

Pink

Pink

Lilac

44

**Purple**

**Brown**

**Dark Yellow**

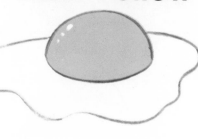

**Light Brown**

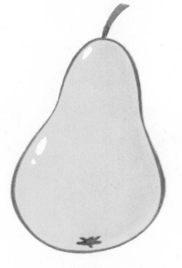

**Green**

**Blue**

**Dark Red**

**Yellow**